El camión de Ana

por Nick Williams
ilustrado por Gaston Vanzet

Harcourt
SCHOOL PUBLISHERS

Cover © Construction Photography

Copyright © by Harcourt, Inc.

All rights reserved. No part of this publication may be reproduced or transmitted in any form or by any means, electronic or mechanical, including photocopy, recording, or any information storage and retrieval system, without permission in writing from the publisher.

Requests for permission to make copies of any part of the work should be addressed to School Permissions and Copyrights, Harcourt, Inc., 6277 Sea Harbor Drive, Orlando, Florida 32887-6777. Fax: 407-345-2418.

HARCOURT and the Harcourt Logo are trademarks of Harcourt, Inc., registered in the United States of America and/or other jurisdictions.

Printed in China

ISBN 10: 0-15-370089-0
ISBN 13: 978-0-15-370089-7

Ordering Options:
ISBN 10: 0-15-368579-4 (ON-LEVEL Collection, Grade 1)
ISBN 13: 978-0-15-368579-8 (ON-LEVEL Collection, Grade 1)
ISBN 10: 0-15-371638-X (package of 5)
ISBN 13: 978-0-15-371638-6 (package of 5)

If you have received these materials as examination copies free of charge, Harcourt School Publishers retains title to the materials and they may not be resold. Resale of examination copies is strictly prohibited and is illegal.

Possession of this publication in print format does not entitle users to convert this publication, or any portion of it, into electronic format.

1 2 3 4 5 6 7 8 9 10 468 16 15 14 13 12 11 10 09 08

Ana está en su camión.

Su camión es grande.

Ana saca algo con
su camión.

4

¿Eso no pesa, Ana?

Ana pone algo con su camión.

6

¡Saca y pone de todo!

Y ahora... ¡a casa!
¡Hasta pronto, Ana!

Submarine

Written by Brylee Gibson

CONTENTS

FINDING A SUBMARINE IN TROUBLE

A submarine can move on the top of the water or deep down at the bottom of the sea. It can stay under the sea for weeks and weeks.

If something goes wrong on a submarine, the people on it might have to be rescued. It can be difficult to rescue the people, but rescuers have special tools to help them.

671

28

a submarine deep under the ocean

3

When a submarine is in trouble, it sends up a beacon. The beacon sends a message by radio. The message tells the rescuers where the submarine is. Rescuers will go to rescue the people.

beacon

Getting to the Submarine

It can take a long time for rescuers to get to a submarine in trouble. Sometimes a diver in a "newtsuit" goes down to let the people on the submarine know that help is coming.

The newtsuit is a suit that people wear if they need to dive deep into the sea. There is enough air inside a newtsuit to last for 48 hours.

newtsuit

The newtsuit is heavy on land, but when it is in the water it is light. The suit is so light that it is easy for the diver to move around. It has legs and arms that can move in different ways. The diver can walk around on the bottom of the sea.

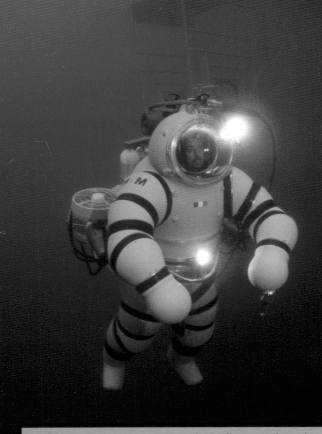

A diver can move around easily wearing the newtsuit.

The diver can look around the outside of the submarine.
The diver can see if the submarine is damaged.
The diver can put air lines between a rescue boat
and the submarine. This will give the people inside some
air until they are rescued.

The diver can also give people on the submarine food
through a special tube.

Getting the People Out

Rescuers sometimes use a small submarine.
This small submarine is called a DSRV.

The people on the submarine must be rescued as soon
as possible, so the DSRV has to get to them quickly. The
DSRV is small enough to be taken to the rescue place
by boat. If it has to be taken to another country, it can be
taken inside an aeroplane.

loading a DSRV onto
an aeroplane

DSRV

MILITARY AIRLIFT COMMAND

WIDE LOAD

11

The DSRV is put in the water. It is taken to the submarine in trouble. The DSRV can only fit 24 people inside, so it may need to make a few trips to rescue everyone.

The DSRV goes to the submarine in trouble on the back of another submarine.

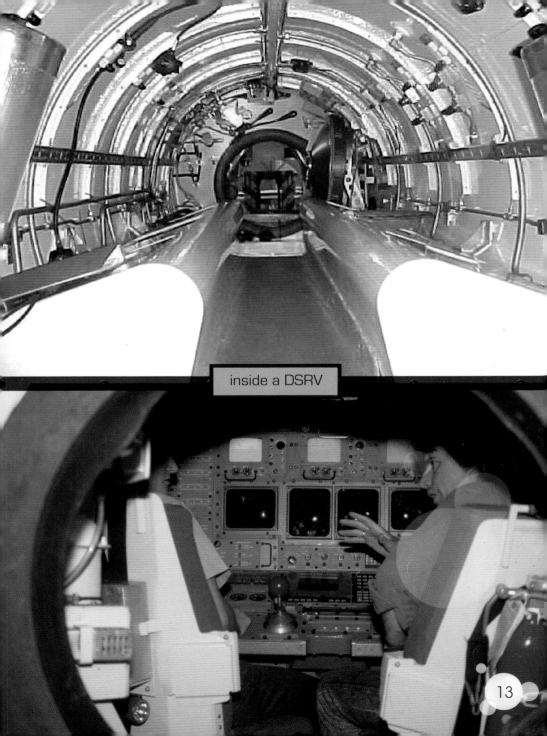

inside a DSRV

It can be very dark at the bottom of the sea and hard for the pilots to see where they are going. The DSRV has special tools that can tell it if anything is in its way. When it reaches the submarine in trouble, it uses a camera to find the escape hatch.

The DSRV drops a tube over the submarine's hatch so that no water can get into the submarine. The hatch can then be opened and the people can climb out.

DSRV

tube over escape hatch

Rescuing people from submarines can be difficult and dangerous work, but with the right tools it can be done safely and quickly.

A submarine in trouble sends up a radio message that tells rescuers where the submarine is.

A diver in a newtsuit helps out while the DSRV is on its way.

The DSRV is taken to the submarine in trouble.

The DSRV drops a tube over the escape hatch and the people can climb out.

INDEX

Reports

Submarine Rescue is a **Report**.

A **report** has a topic:

SUBMARINE RESCUE

A report has headings:

FINDING A SUBMARINE IN TROUBLE

GETTING TO THE SUBMARINE

GETTING THE PEOPLE OUT

Some information is put under headings.

GETTING TO
THE SUBMARINE

A rescue diver can go down to let the people on a submarine know that help is coming.

The rescue diver can look around the outside of the submarine to see if it is damaged.

Information can be shown in other ways.
This report has . . .

Labels   Photographs

Captions   Sequence Chart

Diagrams

DSRV

tube over escape hatch

submarine in trouble

Guide Notes

> **Title:** **Submarine Rescue**
> **Stage:** Fluency
>
> **Text Form:** Informational Report
> **Approach:** Guided Reading
> **Processes:** Thinking Critically, Exploring Language, Processing Information
> **Written and Visual Focus:** Illustrative Diagrams, Labels, Captions, Index,
> Contents Page, Sequence Chart

THINKING CRITICALLY
(sample questions)

Before Reading – Establishing Prior Knowledge
- What do you know about submarine rescues?

Visualising the Text Content
- What might you expect to see in this book?
- What form of writing do you think will be used by the author?

Look at the contents page and index. Encourage the students to think about the information and make predictions about the text content.

After Reading – Interpreting the Text
- What do you think could go wrong on a submarine?
- Why do you think the radio beacon has to stay attached to the submarine?
- Why do you think a newtsuit weighs so much on land and so little in the water?
- Why do you think it is important that people in a submarine are rescued quickly?
- What do you know about submarine rescues that you didn't know before?
- What things in the book helped you understand the information?
- What questions do you have after reading the text?

EXPLORING LANGUAGE

Terminology
Photograph credits, index, contents page, imprint information, ISBN number

Vocabulary
Clarify: beacon, submarine, newtsuit, tube, escape hatch, pilots, DSRV
Nouns: submarine, rescuers, diver
Verbs: sends, walk, climb
Singular/Plural: submarine/submarines, country/countries, hatch/hatches
Focus the students' attention on **adjectives, homonyms, antonyms** and **synonyms** if appropriate